Grassroots
leadership
(4)

compiled by

Michael Hall

Published October 2005 by Island Publications
132 Serpentine Road, Newtownabbey, Co Antrim BT36 7JQ
© Michael Hall 2005
mikeohall@hotmail.com

ISBN 1 899510 67 2

Farset Community Think Tanks Project is funded by:
The EU Special Support Programme for Peace and Reconciliation
administered through the **Northern Ireland Community Relations Council**

Printed by Regency Press, Belfast

Introduction

In Pamphlet No. 63 (*At a new crossroads? An overview of community anxieties*), a veteran community activist remarked that those involved in innovative grassroots activities for the past three decades had never really shared their experiences with a wider audience, especially with the new generation of young people now coming into community work. Accordingly, I conducted a series of interviews with a handful of well-known activists, encouraging them to recount their experiences and reflect on the lessons learned – both positive and negative.

All the interviewees were initially reluctant to reminisce about their experiences, concerned that such personal accounts might read as self-promotion. I endeavoured to assure them of the wider benefit in doing so. Some reminded me that personal accounts were inevitably highly subjective, and that others might have different recollections of the same periods in our history. Nevertheless, despite such anxieties, they all agreed to be interviewed.

These interviews were published in Pamphlets 70, 71 and 72. The feedback from community groups was extremely positive and I was prevailed upon to continue with this approach. Further interviews were therefore conducted for pamphlets 75 and 76.

For this particular pamphlet my interviewees are two individuals who have worked tirelessly for the well-being of their respective communities: well-known Shankill Road community worker **Jackie Redpath**, and, from the other side of the West Belfast interface, recently-retired youth worker **Eilish Reilly**.

Michael Hall *Farset Community Thinks Project*

Jackie Redpath

I was born in the Woodvale area of the Shankill, into an evangelical Christian family who were members of the Shankill Baptist Church (in Tennent Street). I failed the '11-plus' and was sent across town to attend Orangefield. At that time – this was the early 1960s – Orangefield was one of the most progressive secondary schools in Belfast, under the principalship of John Malone. My brother was a teacher and the family decided that Orangefield was the place for me to go. I was the youngest of three children, the other two having passed the '11-plus' – so it was quite a big issue in my family at the time. I remember on my first day at Orangefield that you had to declare your religious denomination. In a state school like Orangefield the 'big three' were Church of Ireland, Presbyterian and Methodist, and for all the rest you were called 'other'. I remember, when asked my denomination, being told to describe myself as 'other'. I think that sense of difference is something that has influenced me all my life.

The evangelical environment in which I grew up was very fundamentalist and it denied me a lot, such as going to football matches or having a TV in the house. You weren't able to go to the pictures, playing cards was out, even playing snooker was a sin. And this also set me apart from my mates. It wasn't that I was lonely; I had friends, but they were doing things that I wasn't allowed to do. Later on, when I had broken away from that upbringing, I became very angry over what I'd been denied. At the same time, I did take out of it the notion of dissent, and it made me connect with the notion of 'Protestant, Catholic and Dissenter'. Because of their 'otherness', the Baptists were dissenters. (It goes way back to the Anabaptists in Münster in Germany, where they set up a commune, and two armies – one ordered by Martin Luther and the other by the Pope – attempted to wipe them out.) That sense of being apart was quite a critical thing in my personal development. I was a wee bit of a preacher in the Baptist Church when I was about 16 or 17. It's ridiculous, I suppose, thinking of a 16/17-year-old standing up preaching to 400 or 600 people and saving souls, but that's what I was doing at that age.

I remember, when asked my denomination, being told to describe myself as 'other'. I think that sense of difference is something that has influenced me all my life.

My journey *out* of Shankill Baptist Church happened after 'The Troubles' broke out. On the Shankill at that time – 1969/70 – there were nightly riots, very, very serious riots, with CS gas and everything... The Baptist Church's response was to move their Sunday night gospel service – the purpose of which was to save souls – from seven o'clock to half four in the afternoon, so that the church people (and their cars) would be out of the way before the riots started. That had a massive affect on me, and I remember thinking: surely that's the time you *need* to be here, especially if you're trying to evangelise, rather than getting out before the trouble starts. I remember going with a couple of other people to the church elders – they'd just built a new church hall in Tennent Street, right at the heart of where the riots were occurring – and saying: 'Look, as you've moved the gospel service forward, would you let us open the church hall and we'll get some of these kids in and talk to them about Jesus?' And they said 'No, we can't do that because it's a new church hall and they'll smoke and put their butts out on the floor' and things like that.

> *I remember thinking: surely that's the time you **need** to be here, especially if you're trying to evangelise, rather than getting out before the trouble starts.*

That was a critical point for me. A few of us broke away from the church and opened a house down in Haddow Street – a small two-up, two-down house – and we called it 'The Way'. We just opened the doors and talked to people about Jesus. And lots of young people the same age as me – I was 18 or 19 at the time – would drop in. It would be called 'peer youth work' or 'detached youth work' now, but, of course, we didn't know about such terms in those days. And they came down and we talked to them about Jesus. The rent of the house was '2 and sixpence' a week, and God paid for it! You just prayed for things and they happened... it's amazing, but you believed it and that was it.

We also connected up with a group – located in Hemel Hempstead of all places – which ran a project which was evangelical but was based out on the streets, and 'The Way' became part of the 'Jesus Liberation Front'. In turn we connected with a guy called Arthur Blessit, an ex-hippie from Los Angeles who was walking around the world carrying a cross on a wheel, and who at one stage camped out in Belfast. At 'The Way' we had crowds of kids coming in who had been barred from youth clubs on the Shankill – in those days you had the YMCA, Agnes Street, St Saviours – and a lot of them got saved and it was a very exciting time. Using one of those old Gestetner duplicating machines we published our own leaflets and went round pubs and clubs, talking to people about Jesus. And all the time the riots were going on all around us, so it was quite remarkable.

I started to see the irrelevance of the established churches. Even the Baptist church, while not a mainstream church, still wasn't connecting. But our project *did* offer a way of connecting and I was into it big time. In the 'Jesus Liberation Front' we were doing all sorts of things and going places Christians had never gone, and talking to different people and publishing leaflets and so on. We even went charismatic at one point: all this speaking in tongues and healing and stuff. We linked up with Clonard, where there were charismatic Catholics, and about 60 of us from the Shankill used to walk through the 'no-go' areas right into Clonard.

In 1972 I was also attending Queen's University. Through the good education I had received at Orangefield I ended up getting A-levels and then getting into Queen's to do History. But, to be honest, I didn't really go there all that much because I was so heavily into my Jesus Liberation Front work. So, yet again, although I was at Queen's I was a Christian and I didn't fit in, didn't drink or anything like that. Maybe that's the story of my life: being a part of a group but yet also being apart from that group. I ended up getting my degree, but for me at that time The Jesus Liberation Front was much more exciting than Queens.

Alongside this you had the growing conflagration that was happening on the ground, with the 'no-go' areas and all that type of thing. A lot of young people signed up for paramilitary organisations, particularly the UDA, just because everybody else did. But when some of these young people got saved through our work, that was when we first learned negotiation skills, because we had to try and get them out of those organisations.

But then I noticed something happening. The kids who came to the house were all a bit mad and often very rough. After all, they had been barred from the local youth clubs, and many were members of the gangs which existed at that time, like the Tartan gangs and the 'Rats'. Anyway, the kids that got saved or became Christians started going upstairs in the house to pray and talk, while the other ones, the rough ones who didn't get saved, were left downstairs – and a definite separation developed between the two groups. And I sort of got more interested in the ones downstairs than the ones that were upstairs praying. And then one day the ones that were downstairs arrived with all these doors which they had taken off old houses that were getting demolished, and they started making window boxes out of the wood. And the whole of

My attitudes gradually changed. I no longer saw the relevance of the way I'd been brought up and the established churches in the Shankill to the mayhem that was going on around me.

Sugarfield Street and Bellview Street were given window boxes by these supposedly wild kids who wouldn't become Christians. They made other window boxes and sold them to people – an early 'social economy business'.

At the time I'd started to get into different sorts of theology – South American Liberation theology and stuff like that. And my attitudes gradually changed. I no longer saw the relevance of the way I'd been brought up and the established churches in the Shankill to the mayhem that was going on around me. And I don't just mean the Troubles – with the riots, the 'no-go' areas, and guns on the streets – but the wholesale redevelopment that was taking place. That was the most awful experience in people's lives: homes were compulsorily purchased, bulldozers moved in and they just knocked down entire streets, some of it because of the needs of a proposed new ring road (only part of which was completed and is now known as the Westlink). Great swathes of the Shankill were affected. I mean, the contracts for demolition on the Shankill were for 500 houses at a time. And I started thinking: this is what's happening in people's lives, yet the churches are not relating to it, they're irrelevant. I suppose my thinking was moving into seeing things more from a social perspective than a religious one.

In 1973 I had left Queen's University, got married and was renting a house in the Hammer, in Mansfield Street. I set about looking for a job but wasn't too successful at first. And then a job came up with the Shankill Community Council, with the grand title of 'Secretary Organiser', and I applied for it and got it. The Shankill Community Council at that point was a coming together of church people, some community people, youth workers and so on – people like Rev. Bill Jackson, Mina Wardle, Annie Morrison and Brian Smeaton. I got that job in 1974, and was soon involved in

I had moved from a Christian-driven motivation to a social/community-driven one and felt: this is where I belong. And I had a passion for it and a belief in it.

major protests about housing and other community issues. I was still involved in 'The Way', but by this stage I'd lost contact with the church. I had moved from a Christian-driven motivation to a social/community-driven one and felt: this is where I belong. And I had a passion for it and a belief in it.

The 'system' – in terms of the government and the Housing Executive, as with the Belfast Corporation before it – was absolutely wrecking the Shankill and during the three years 1974-77 the first highlight of my life in community work was the 'Save the Shankill' campaign. That arose out of work I'd done with an academic called Ron Wiener, who wrote *The Rape and Plunder of the Shankill*, which is still a book used on university courses. Ron's study highlighted the devastating impact which badly-conceived redevelopment was having on the Shankill – both in terms of its housing stock and its people. There was one particular critical point for me. On behalf of the Shankill Community Council we were attempting to negotiate with the Housing Executive about what they were building on the Shankill, to replace the demolished old houses. Before I had got involved on the issue, the Executive had already built the 'Weetabix'† flats in the Lower Shankill. Indeed, most of the Lower Shankill estate had been rebuilt and it was an absolute disaster. And now they were moving on up into Percy Street and intending to do the same thing there: they had nine blocks of flats planned for there. This was to be my first experience of confrontation with the Housing Executive.

† So-called because the surface of the walls crumbled when rubbed.

Along with Ron Wiener and Claire Curry, who was an outreach youth worker for the YMCA, we met with Housing Executive planners. One of them was a man who actually came from the top of the Shankill. I often found in dealing with planners that the worst ones were those who had some connection with working-class roots, because they thought they knew better. At the meeting I said: 'Look, this idea of building nine blocks of flats is all wrong.' We argued for terraced housing to be built instead. And this guy said, in effect: 'Look, 120 years ago when the Shankill was built nobody was used to terrace housing, but they got used to it. They'll get used to these flats; now go away and leave me alone.' And that was the end of the meeting – there was no negotiation. I was feeling really angry and as a result of that meeting the 'Save the Shankill' campaign was set up.

I realised that the Shankill Community Council alone didn't have clout and so, alongside the Community Council, we brought representatives of the churches, the Shankill Traders' Association and the paramilitary organisations – the UVF, the Orange Volunteers, the UDA, and an organisation called Women's Action which was connected to the UDA. These different interest groups were brought together under the 'Save the Shankill' campaign. Now, this was late 1974, and the Ulster Workers Council strike had taken place in May, so we went to the UWC and approached a guy called Jim Smyth to be our chairman, while I became secretary.

I'll never forget the excitement that resulted from the intense protests we organised throughout the next five or six years. It's too detailed a story to go into here, but we did everything and anything to stymie the planners, and eventually we forced them to change their plans. Indeed, we actually got to a point where we could trust the Housing Executive to do the thing right. I would argue that the 'Save the Shankill' campaign, in terms of the British Isles, was one of the most successful community action campaigns ever undertaken.

And I would want that to stand as one of my proudest moments. That, in the middle of the mayhem caused by 'The Troubles', redevelopment, the economic collapse of major industries – the Shipyard, Mackies and others – in the middle of all that, the 'Save the Shankill' campaign *did* save the Shankill, certainly at that point. I don't want to overclaim

> *I would argue that the 'Save the Shankill' campaign, in terms of the British Isles, was one of the most successful community action campaigns ever undertaken.*

it, but I'd argue that it would be a very different place today if it weren't for that campaign. So I think that's probably my proudest involvement in terms of community.

I left the Community Council in 1977, in the middle of all this, because I was getting weighed down with sub-committees and administrative stuff, and I was young, had just married, kids arriving... After a year's unemployment I started working for the Shankill Education Workshop, which sought to determine what was happening on the Shankill educationally. We opened up this radical adult education project. Nowadays adult education is an accepted thing, but there wasn't any of it about then, certainly not on the Shankill. We set up classes and began to put education on the agenda. We also began to publish a small A4-sized newspaper – called the *Shankill Bulletin* – using it to promote community activities and attack what the government was doing to the Shankill. The Department of Education, who were funding the Workshop, eventually withdrew their funding in 1979/80. But a diverse group of people had come together around the Workshop: local people, ex-prisoners, pensioners, some professional people, and individuals from the likes of VSB (Voluntary Service Bureau) and the Centre for Neighbourhood Development.

Another individual who got very much involved was Buzz Logan, originally a staff photographer for the *Irish Independent* in Dublin. He had been doing some work of his own in the slum areas of Dublin, and a local teacher who happened to know him suggested he come up and look around the Shankill. I remember the day he came; he said: 'This is just like the place that I'm operating in down in Dublin.' And so he started taking photographs of the Shankill. Buzz actually ended up leaving his job in Dublin – which was well paid with big expenses – to set up the Shankill Photographic Workshop within the Education Workshop, and he also took photos for the *Shankill Bulletin*.

> *The* **Shankill Bulletin...** *was published from 1983 to 1989. We brought it out it monthly, sometimes fortnightly, and it was a brilliant experience, the second highlight of my working life on the Shankill.*

But when the funding was withdrawn we were faced with a dilemma. If we were going to have to raise funds to keep all the different projects going we knew we'd end up spending most of our time fund-raising and less and less on the actual projects. We asked ourselves if there was something within what we were doing which we should focus on, and we decided to concentrate on the newspaper. We turned the *Shankill Bulletin* from an A4 print-out into a tabloid. And it was published from 1983 to 1989 – eventually changing its title to *The Shankill People*. We brought it out monthly, sometimes fortnightly, and it was a brilliant experience, the second highlight of my working life on the Shankill.

'The Troubles' were at their peak and the paper stood for progressive Unionist politics. If anyone wants to read copies they're all in the Linen Hall Library. Although we used to do a free issue at Christmas it was basically sold through local shops. But you never knew at the end of each week whether there'd be anything in the bank or not for wages. Sometimes there was, other times there wasn't – but you carried on anyway. We received no government funding whatsoever. Sometimes you'd hit a trust for a grant of maybe a couple of thousand pounds. I remember we got a grant for £6000 and that sustained us for a year, but it wasn't a really a sustainable enterprise on its own.

I should point out that throughout all this time there were always contacts being established across the 'divide'. I remember the whole issue over Divis Flats, about whether they should be demolished or not, then the campaign against the ring road, and all the work done with Jim McCorry. And you found that people on the Shankill had as radical an agenda as people on the other side of the peaceline in West Belfast. It never formed up into structured organisations which were cross-community, but there was an awful lot of joint work done. And the joy of it was that it happened quite naturally, it never had to be engineered – I mean, this is long before cross-community funding made its appearance – it was because there were issues that were common to both the Shankill and the Falls.

During that time, another spin-off was the North and West Belfast Federation of Tenants' Associations, which was a Greater Shankill Association incorporating tenants' groups from Lower Shankill, right up through Ainsworth, to Glencairn, Springmartin, Highfield, and then stretching up to Silverstream, Benview, Tynedale, Sunningdale... and we brought this amalgam of groups together. And that was the late 70s, early 80s. One of the big issues was the rent increase the Housing Executive was demanding. We organised a rent strike, took over Housing Executive offices, and published our own tenants' association newssheet. Over three or four years we fought what you would call a community action campaign. That was a brilliant organisation as well, another high point for me.

The Troubles have thrown up some particularly intense and horrific periods. One such commenced with the 'Gibraltar Three' being shot dead, followed by Michael Stone's attack on the mourners at Milltown Cemetery, then the horror in West Belfast of the two corporals being dragged from their car and murdered. Now, there had been plenty of soldiers and others murdered before, the difference here was that these two were murdered in front of the TV cameras, they were virtually crucified. So over a very short period you had this conflagration in West Belfast and graffiti appeared saying: 'Welcome to Beirut'. And it really did seem as if we were going down the route of Beirut. The SDLP, the Catholic Church, the Irish Government... had all lost any sort of semblance of relevance to what was happening in West Belfast. And at that point the British government launched this initiative, the Belfast Action Teams, with the theme 'Making Belfast Work'. Actually, its first title was 'Making West Belfast Work' for it was very much a Catholic West Belfast initiative. And I remember some of us on the Shankill putting our hands up and saying: 'Hold on, disadvantage doesn't belong to one community here.' Or as Hughie Smyth – who has worked consistently as a councillor throughout all this – said:

And the joy of it was that [this cross-community work] happened quite naturally, it never had to be engineered – it was because there were issues that were common to both the Shankill and the Falls.

'Poverty knows no religion.' So we got the Shankill put on the agenda with the Belfast Action Teams (BAT).

However, this also marked the first signs of community fragmentation in the Shankill, because what you found with the civil servants who were the BAT leaders was that if they liked you they gave you money, and if they didn't like you they didn't. Furthermore, what was happening in Catholic West Belfast was that government was pumping money into Catholic Church-driven organisations in an attempt to isolate Sinn Féin, hoping to regain some control of the situation at community level. And the BAT leader, whose experience had been working in Catholic West Belfast, and who was a good man, just brought that experience to the Shankill, and went for the churches and other 'safe people' basically. Part of this development saw the establishment of the Greater Shankill Development Agency. I was still doing the *Shankill People* at the time, but with four kids and all sorts of responsibilities, I thought I'd better look for a job that paid a proper wage, and when one came up with the Greater Shankill Development Agency, I applied and got it. This was in 1989.

But a critical point arose – this was in 1992 – when we said: This isn't about another six good projects, or six good ideas, surely this is about this community thinking 20 years ahead?

What had been happening at community level at that time was a move, if you like, 'from protests to projects'. The whole protest experience, involving issues such as the 'Save the Shankill' campaign and the agitation undertaken by the North and West Belfast Federation of Tenants' Associations, had given way to a new approach. There were things set up such as Woodvale and Shankill Housing Association, and various youth workshops were established, such as Woodvale Youth Training Project – which became Farset – under Jackie Hewitt, Crumlin Road Opportunities Ltd., and others. And all these projects sought to address housing, employment and numerous other issues. But now, with the arrival of BAT, there was an increasing move from individual projects to more all-embracing development, and the Greater Shankill Development Agency was involved in that. Argyle Business Centre was established, we put education on the agenda and a whole range of things were set in place, some of them good, some of them not so good. You would usually get three years' funding and would sit down to look at what half dozen projects or ideas you were going to focus on. And you knew that would be repeated with the next funding tranche was due – you would sit down to think of another six things to do.

But a critical point arose – this was in 1992 – when we said: This isn't about another six good projects, or six good ideas, surely this is about this community thinking *20 years* ahead, on the basis that if *we* don't do that, either somebody else is going to shape it for the next 20 years, ie. government, or else they'll not bother and it will just be shapeless and left to stagnate. The only alternative was for the community to try and shape its own future. And it was that concept of trying to shape the future that made the Shankill, as far as I am aware, the first community in Northern Ireland to move away from a focus on short-term projects to a long-term strategy.

And in 1993-94 we set about developing a long-term strategy, a regeneration strategy. We'd had redevelopment in the 70s, rehabilitation in the 80s, and we were now into regeneration. So the next big point – and my most fulfilling two years I think, apart from the 'Save The Shankill' years – was in 1993-94 when we were developing that strategy and identifying the key issues. It was a very intensive period, we'd hundreds of people involved in discussions and debates, and through that we identified those areas that we felt required development – such as education, training, employment, housing, sport, economic infrastructure, and health – a whole range of areas critical to the future of the community. And, finally, as a result of those intense discussions with hundreds of people, over a two-year period, we determined that education was the critical element in terms of the future of the Shankill.

We felt that if we could get education right everything else would take care of itself. Although, having said that, we knew that you couldn't just concentrate on any one issue, because if you got the education right and people suddenly started achieving qualifications, there needed to be well-paid jobs available for them, and there also needed to be decent housing for them to buy otherwise they were going to move out of the area. So we knew that not only did we need to get the education right, but we also had to get the housing right and the jobs right. However, if you just concentrated on jobs – which was the big government push at the time under the BAT teams – and managed to get firms to set up within the Shankill the reality was that local people wouldn't have got those jobs anyway, because they didn't have either the education or the training. So it had to be a holistic approach, but with education at its centre. And the primary outcome was the Early Years Project, where we got 100 local people employed whose task was to help develop the parenting skills of families with new-born children, in an effort to stimulate a whole new

And it was that concept of trying to shape the future that made the Shankill, as far as I am aware, the first community in Northern Ireland to move away from a focus on short-term projects to a long-term strategy.

positive approach to education. And that experience has been absolutely brilliant.

Furthermore, out of this period of analysis came the notion that the community has the ideas and knows what is needed, while the government and their departments and agencies have the money, and the best way to marry the two is through a partnership. And from that developed the Greater Shankill Partnership, where representatives of government and community could, supposedly, work together for the good of the Greater Shankill.

Now I'm fairly convinced that partnership is the way forward and I hold to it because I believe in it, but partnership between government and community isn't easy, it's a rocky road. And, furthermore, over the last number of years it has resulted in community fragmentation in the Shankill, which, apart from the feud, has been the most painful experience in my life, when you had people who had worked together for years now not working together. Fortunately, the fragmentation got healed, partly as a result of the feud in 2000, although it was actually healing before that.

As for the feud in August 2000... I've talked so far about the high points, but the feud – along with the 'Shankill Bomb' in October 1993 – was the lowest point for me, because it's changed the community that I grew up in and worked in beyond recognition – it's not the same place that I knew. That feud, and then what happened after it in terms of the various infightings within the UDA and so forth in 2002... had a devastating impact on community morale. The one thing I always believed

> *The [Loyalist] feud was the lowest point for me, because it's changed the community that I grew up in and worked in beyond recognition – it's not the same place that I knew.*

about the Shankill was that it didn't matter what you did to it – 'The Troubles', redevelopment, whatever – the spirit of the people would remain intact, and it would bounce back. For the Shankill is more than a place, it's a people, and the spirit of the people was always there. What that feud did was break that spirit and even today it's still not the community that I knew. Now, we've tried to struggle through that, and coming out of all that was the Shankill Convention. And that has made real efforts to bring the community together, and, in effect, give the Shankill back to the people. Sometimes it's painted as something that arose because of the feud in an effort to try and get the paramilitaries together, and certainly that was part of it, but the Convention was really an attempt to give the Shankill back to the people.

And it's an ongoing effort. Momentum has gone up and down over the last three years. But we've achieved significant things, in terms of the housing strategy and the excellent exhibitions that have been organised showcasing all the good work that has gone on in this community. And more recently (June 2005) the Convention was together again, saying let's get back to a regeneration agenda, and that's a great joy. It's not flawless, but it's there, and it's trying to deal with issues of community fragmentation. The problem is that once money comes into the picture it's divisive, and there have been things that have stretched the Convention, but we're still there, we're still on the street, and we're going to be there.

At the moment, my feeling is that the Shankill's very existence is no longer under threat. Back in 1977 I have no doubt, and it's documented, that there was a plot to eradicate the Shankill. And I am *not* conspiratorial by nature, but I've no doubt that at one point in the mid-70s, when 'The Troubles' were at their height, the British military decided that it would be much easier to deal with a situation where an East Belfast Protestant community was separated by the River Lagan from a West Belfast Catholic community. That's putting it in crude terms, but that's what I think they would have preferred. And a lot of the redevelopment efforts, which decimated the old Shankill, seemed to be part of that push to eliminate this uncontrollable thorn in the side of the security forces.

I don't think the Shankill's physical existence is threatened now, especially when you see private housing being developed right beside the peaceline – and actually selling. What I am not sure of is whether the Shankill will change sufficiently to meet the new challenges. So while it might have a guaranteed future, in the physical sense, will the spirit of the community survive, will it be a better place for people to live in and to work in? We have a great potential to press the self-destruct buttons.

I also think the Shankill's future is mirrored in the future of Unionism, and the Protestant community's sense of belief in itself has been badly shaken. Although I have been a supporter of the Good Friday Agreement, in the period since then people on the Shankill have increasingly felt they were on the losing side, especially when they saw both symbolic and real gains being made by Republicanism, without any evidenced compensatory gains by Unionism. They felt that the tide was largely turning against them and that the 'other side' were making all the gains. And then, to compound that deep sense of loss and alienation, came the feud, and that absolutely wrecked things. We're still trying to recover from its legacy. And it also undoubtedly served to undermine the attempts made by myself and others – particularly in America from 1994 onwards – to build a better international understanding of the Protestant community, Unionism and working-class issues.

I also think the Shankill's future is mirrored in the future of Unionism, and the Protestant community's sense of belief in itself has been badly shaken.

Yet I have to believe that, *despite* all these things and despite the damage that has been wrought, the spirit of the people is still there somewhere and that's what we need to try and get hold off. However, to be honest, I feel it needs better people than me to do that, and my greatest joy would be to see a new generation of younger people on the Shankill coming through to get hold of that spirit and take it forward.

And they *are* there, although whether they're able to come through or not is another question. Many of our most prominent community activists go back to the 60s and 70s, and the way they came into 'community work' was mainly though voluntary effort. People went to their everyday jobs and then came out and did their community work at night, or did so during the day by taking time off. These days your *only* route in – and this isn't the fault of today's young people – is professionally, and with the necessary qualifications. There's a lot of people in key positions on the Shankill probably wouldn't get those jobs today if they had to apply for them – they got them through voluntary effort and sheer commitment and staying power. Nowadays you only get the job if you've got the qualifications, and once you get the job, that job is professionalised and constrained within the cage of whatever organisation is employing you. Now, these people do great work... there's stuff happening in the Shankill today that is world class, some of it happening nowhere else – and we need to remember that – but a lot of those people are still constrained within a project-led, qualification-demanding professionalism. And the younger people, who are out there in their dozens on the Shankill, might not get a look in unless they can follow that same professional, qualification-driven path.

I have great hopes in our young people – not only young people on the Shankill, but young people from *all* our communities. Although my core job is focused on the needs of the Shankill, I am involved in cross-community work, which is also important to me. For example, I am Chair of Springboard, which is a Wider Horizons Programme funded by the IFI (International Fund for Ireland) which brings together young Protestant and Catholic young people from Belfast, as well as young people from Dublin, and widens their horizons through international work placements – in Canada, the USA, Europe, South Africa and elsewhere.

Our young people possess great potential. So I hope that they do manage to get involved in community work, and that they can move in and take over the territory that people like me were in.

Our young people possess great potential. So I hope that they *do* manage to get involved in community work, and that they can move in and take over the territory that people like me were in. I want out, I've done my best, but I want out, and no greater joy would it give me than somebody tapping me on the shoulder and saying: 'Come on, Jackie, time for you to go... we're doing it now.'

Eilish Reilly

I was born in 1942, the eldest of a family of nine. I had six brothers and two sisters and we were reared in Slate Street. I went to Balkan Street school, and then to St Dominic's. At that time most people left school at 14 years of age, and, finding it strange whenever the young people I grew up with were going out working, I left St Dominic's and went into a dressmaking firm in Great Victoria Street – Ellison Brothers. I had a very happy childhood and very happy teenage years. And when I went to work in Ellison's I worked with Protestants and Catholics and had as many Protestant girlfriends as I had Catholic ones – and we all went to the dances and had a good time together.

And then my family moved to the Glen Road. I was only there about two and a half years when I got married, and moved into Dermot Hill and have lived here ever since. It was just shortly after we moved here that the Civil Rights movement started, then all the civil unrest, and gradually it just developed into a war situation. My fourth child was born a week before Bloody Sunday (1972), so my family was being brought up in an area that was actually in the middle of it all. (I have five children and ten grandchildren.) It was happening all over, of course, but there were so many things taking place in this area that people felt as if they were being confined: you were in an area and that was it, you couldn't really move out of it.

At one particular stage, in 1972, there was a building put up on the mountain 'loaney' [lane] – and this was 'Newhill'. It was supposed to be a youth and community centre but to be quite honest it was really only four walls made with breezeblocks and a roof, there was absolutely nothing in it. I can't remember

There were so many things taking place in this area that people felt as if they were being confined: you were in an area and that was it, you couldn't really move out of it.

who put it up but a ten-year-old girl across the street, Noreen Cummings, had been very eager to get it built, and she was all excited, saying: 'It's great, it will be somewhere for us to go, but what we need is volunteers, we need adults to help to run it.' And Noreen encouraged me to come over and help out, and I encouraged my next door neighbour to go with me.

So we went over and the young people were doing their best at a bit of fundraising. But, really, it was just one big empty space, and there were no youth leaders there – it was just put up and left for the community to run it. I helped out for a while and then I faded out of things, before being approached by another person, Phyllis Little, who was trying to keep things going and asked me to do some more voluntary work. So I started going over again, but, to be honest, I still wasn't all that much interested.

However, everything was sort of happening in the area, and there were many men – and women – interned, including my husband. And it seemed to be that the women in the community were being left not only to be both mother and father to their own children but also to look out for the safety of all the children in the area. And there was nothing for young people to do or nowhere to go.

In fact, this place, Newhill, was the only thing that we had going in this area, so I went over for another short while to help out. Then I was approached by Bridie McClure, who told me that she was meeting with some women from Dermott Hill to discuss the future of Newhill, and would I come along. And the women who were there all seemed very determined that we had to do something for our community, because the situation was getting worse and our children were all growing up confined in their own area – many of them rarely got into the centre of the town. So we sat down and we talked and, as I said, there was a whole new determination among the women, and before that night ended every person in that room went away with a job to do.

We also met with a group of women from New Barnsley who were interested in making a success of Newhill, so that everyone would benefit from its presence. We wanted to involve as many people as

We also decided to undertake some training, just to see what was involved in youth work, for we knew there was more to it than standing about making sure young people didn't start fights with one another.

possible to tackle the different issues within our communities, to empower people at a grassroots level. So then we finally started to put some real structure into what was going on in Newhill. Previously it was mostly a case of us volunteers just supervising while the young people ran their discos and such things, but nothing really structured.

We were acting not only as the management committee but working with the young people at the same time. We drew up a weekly programme, where we said: 'Now, from Monday to Sunday, what will we do with this youth club and how can we make it better for the people of the area?' Newhill itself had a very high ceiling, it was always freezing cold, and wasn't very welcoming for women or young babies. But the youth wanted it – in fact, the youth *needed* it – so the majority of things that took place were geared towards them. And gradually we were able to add different activities: a boxing club, a football club, a swimming club, a dance programme, discos of course, and general activities.

We also decided to undertake some training, just to see what was involved in youth work, for we knew there was more to it than standing about making sure young people didn't start fights with one another. So we went and did our Stage 1 in Youth and Community Work – and that gave you a new insight so that you could start to develop a vision for the future and the way you wanted your community to develop, as well as things that you could get the young people involved in. But in a way in which the young people were included in all the decision-making within what was, after all, their own club.

Because as the years went by and the Troubles intensified many of the young people felt marginalised and alienated from their communities and they got into continual trouble with paramilitaries. A lot of things were happening in their lives, just as a lot of things weren't happening, so we decided that we would focus on giving young people a bigger part to play, within their own communities, within their own youth club, getting them to take responsibility for their actions, involving them in planning their own programmes and sharing the knowledge that we had and the experiences that we had with them – sort of skilling them up to do things for themselves. And letting them know that we as adults valued them, and wanted them to be part of the community and wanted them to be involved from volunteer right up to management level, you know. So we went about all that and it was very, very successful. Tracie McKee, one of our youth workers, worked tirelessly to ensure that young people participated fully at all levels, planning and implementing programmes for the children and young people. For their part, the young people showed leadership and responsibility.

A girl called Anne O'Neill came along and showed us how to submit our first grant application and we wrote away to Children in Need who gave us money for equipment – they are still supporting us to this day. Encouraged by that, we started to search out other funders and also began to network with other youth clubs and community centres in West Belfast to see what was happening with them. And we were gradually building up our skills base and our knowledge of what was available out there, and we were getting quite good at it.

But in the meantime, while we were strengthening our ability to develop our own community, the building itself was falling asunder. A skylight window blew off and let the rain in, so every night we had to sweep out the water before we could let the young people in. Sometimes we could only use half the floor space, and it was always freezing. At one stage we were actually going to close it down altogether, but the young people insisted that they'd nowhere else to go. We were in negotiations with Belfast City Council and BELB [Belfast Education & Library Board], but there were various difficulties as to whether Newhill was a youth club or a community centre, or both, because this was important with regards to funding.

> *The building itself was falling asunder. A skylight window blew off and let the rain in, so every night we had to sweep out the water before we could let the young people in. And it was always freezing.*

To combat the cold, some of us actually used to bring over our own Super Sers [bottled gas heaters] to the club… and when you got a group of young people around them it was great to sit and listen, just in a wee cosy corner, to what these young people were saying. Through these wee groups and listening

18

to young people I became very interested in what they had to say and what their needs were and what they wanted to do. And during this time I built up really great relationships with many young people.

We struggled on for a number of years until Frank Cahill introduced us to Kate Kelly from BAT [Belfast Action Teams]. Kate was invited up and she was amazed at the work that was going on inside the club despite the terrible conditions we were working under. She gave us the money to undertake a whole new refurbishment – only the original foundations were kept. Instead of one big room there were now two rooms – a big one and a smaller one – and the kitchen was renovated and the boxing suite done up. The new club had its official opening in July 1990.

Everything in Newhill came from grants. We were continually fund-raising. We just had to sit down and get to know who the funders were, and who would fund what... it was a constant exercise. Just as it was to look after the young people's needs, to keep them occupied, to stop them from getting into trouble, to give them some kind of social outlet. Because there was absolutely nothing whatsoever for them to do. This was the place where they met, the place where they had a bit of craic, the place where they could come in out of the cold to keep warm – the new building was nice and warm and welcoming.

It was a constant exercise... to look after the young people's needs, to keep them occupied, to stop them from getting into trouble, to give them some kind of social outlet. Because there was absolutely nothing whatsoever for them to do.

I worked very closely with Maura Fryers, Geraldine O'Reagan, Mary McGlade and Bridie McClure in the youth club. Then Bridie, who had been such a great inspiration to us at the very beginning, departed for America. Geraldine moved into community development, and she applied for the job of Director while Maura applied to manage the pre-school playgroup. I became the Leader in Charge of the youth club. Mary still works in the community.

In saying that, in all the years before these new jobs came in nearly everything was voluntary – all those years we worked in a voluntary capacity. BELB gave us the equivalent of one youth worker's wage – in the form of a grant for ten months per year – and to this day that hasn't changed, we're still only getting that. Nevertheless, Newhill has been one of the most successful youth clubs around for a long while. When the European 'peace money' came in we were given the funding for the post of Youth Co-ordinator and I was successful. I worked for three years in that post and then we got a two-year extension. We successfully applied for the next tranche of EU funding [Peace II] but by that time I felt I'd done what I set out to do, and wanted to retire from youth work. Well, sort of retire, because I was involved in so many different things. There's a young fella at the moment, Phillip Glennon, who's now the Young People's Development Officer, and he's doing a great job. Paul Lappin is Leader in

Charge, and one of the most reliable youth workers I have worked with.

During all those years there's been an awful lot of young people in this area who have had problems. Apart from the Troubles-related problems, there was high unemployment, health issues, poor housing, an awful lot of disadvantage, no amenities... the whole community needed to be developed. And it was our vision to do this when the new building was opened in 1990. We were able to get ACE [Action for Community Employment] jobs, and although many people didn't like ACE, at least it meant you could get people working for a year at a time, which allowed you to build up projects. We set up a creche, a pre-school playgroup, then an after-schools club, a homework club, and within the youth club itself there was a boxing club and a football club. In the new building we were better organised because we had separate rooms to do different things in.

I suppose the most important thing I did when I was leader was to *listen* to what young people were saying, and to respond to their needs. But also to encourage them to participate in everything that they wanted to see done – to give them responsibility. For instance, there was this big issue going on one time about young people hanging round street corners – which is still a big issue everywhere. Residents were getting them to move away from their houses, but when they went down to the other end of the street, residents there moved them on again. And it wasn't that they were drinking or whatever, they were just hanging about, for the majority of the young people just had nowhere to go. The youth club would close around 10 o'clock at night but the young people maybe hung around to half eleven or whatever. And there was a big outcry about young people getting into trouble. Now, I was working with this group of young people who called themselves the Newhill Youth Development Team, who were elected on a yearly basis and spoke for the young people and for their needs. They arranged a meeting between the young people who were hanging around corners and the residents, and it went really well. The young people told the residents their problems, and the residents told them *their* problems.

I suppose the most important thing I did when I was leader was to **listen** *to what young people were saying, and to respond to their needs. But also to encourage them to participate in everything that they wanted to see done – to give them responsibility.*

So what came out of that was the idea for a youth café, and the young people themselves wrote away to the Millennium Trust – part of the National Lottery – and they got £16,000 to open up a café.

Now this youth café was run by young people with the support of two youth leaders and they opened their doors after the youth club closed in the evening. And it was very successful: a lot of young people who were marginalised and who were hanging around corners and who didn't even use the youth club were invited in to participate in the events that took place.

The Newhill Youth Development Team itself was absolutely brilliant. The young members of the Team went out and spoke to other young people on the street corners and it went from strength to strength. Not only did they invite the young people to come into the café, they got them involved in other projects. Other youth club leaders came to see what way it was working, intending to set up similar projects. The Team organised training for themselves, and for other young people, and got involved on different management committees. And when they sat down and did a Think Tank pamphlet†, a lot more people were made aware of the different issues faced by young people in these areas.

As well as being involved in issues specifically concerning Newhill Youth Club, I have been involved in a lot of other projects which had a wider impact. I was in a group that was involved in setting up the Play Resource Warehouse, the others being Monina O'Prey, Moya Hynes, Anne O'Kelly (who, as Anne O'Neill, had showed us how to do our first application), and Robert Martin. Because Newhill, at that particular time, was so bleak and desolate looking we used to bring over all these odds and ends from our own homes to let the children do arts and crafts. Anyway, we sat down one time and, knowing that

The Newhill Youth Development Team itself was absolutely brilliant. Other youth clubs came to see what way it was working and went way intending to set up similar projects.

other clubs must be in the same situation, thought that it would be really good to have a central base where playgroups and youth groups could come and obtain bits of material and stuff discarded by the big shops and warehouses. For instance, I recalled that in Ellison's, where I had worked, there would often be lots of bits of material thrown out.

So we came up with the idea of asking warehouses and firms to supply us with any *safe* material that they discarded. Then the City Council was approached, and they told us to look for a base – in which to store all this stuff – which would be neutral and would serve both communities. And we ended up with a big warehouse in Tomb Street – and the work that we had to put into that! I don't know what it was before we got it, it was either a birdseed place or a fish-food thing, but the smell of it! We had to scrub walls and everything. But it ended up very successful and today is still a great success. Community groups from all over have used it, and community workers from as far away as Sligo have come to see how it worked. When the lease of the Tomb Street premises expired the Play Resource Warehouse moved to the Antrim Road, and then they got a big grant from the National Lottery. It's an absolutely fantastic community resource. So I was involved in that, I was a trustee and we got it done up and there was a big opening day for it. We had ACE workers back then, but today the staff sustain their own salaries.

† Island Pamphlet No. 20 *Young People Speak Out*, 1999.

I was also involved in helping to set up a peer education programme, which focused on the many health problems facing young people. It was initially run from the Whiterock Health Centre. But then a lot of money – £6M – came into this area and the Upper Springfield Development Trust was set up, so the peer educators became part of that programme. And now I hear that they've gone mainstream. So that's another success story.

I was also involved in the Upper Springfield Youth Network, which was an attempt to bring all the local youth clubs together, and three times a year they organise three big events. Now, they've done some fantastic stuff, and it means that the youth leaders can meet up and support each other, and they do inter-club visits. Another great character I worked with, who was also a youth leader, was Tommy Slavin.

We also had this great initiative on the go – a caravan project which was fantastic. Stuart Kennedy – who was at university at the time – had come to work alongside me and had this great idea for establishing contact with the young people who weren't getting involved in Newhill, or in any club; those who felt alienated even from their own communities and were being called 'anti-social' and what have you. His idea was to get a caravan and *bring* it to the very places where these young people hung out. We were uncertain at first. After all, there was always the possibility that we would maybe get stoned or chased away! But anyway, we went ahead. We had access to a minibus and we used to tow the caravan up to the young people who stood at the top of the mountain loaney and various other locations where young people hung out.

There was a bit of a programme going on inside the caravan, making young people aware of the dangers of things like drugs. There was a wee stove in the caravan, and the young people would get a cup of tea and a biscuit. And as the young people got to know where it would be on a particular night – it might be outside the Fort† or it might be elsewhere – instead of hanging round corners, they actually congregated wherever this caravan was. At one time a leader from another club came to see what it was all about, and I says: 'It's up the mountain loaney tonight, we'll take a walk up and see what's happening.' And when we went up he was amazed. The minibus was full of young people – there was a youth leader in the minibus running a youth programme – and the caravan was full also. And there were young people

The minibus was full of young people – there was a youth leader in the minibus running a youth programme – and the caravan was full also. And there were young people standing in between the caravan and the minibus, just chatting together. It was a very successful project.

† A reference to the huge British Army base, 'Fort Whiterock' (but known to local people as 'Fort Jericho' because of the frequency with which parts of the perimeter fencing would fall down), on the Springfield Road which overlooked the entire area, The base was eventually demolished.

standing in between the caravan and the minibus, just chatting together. It was a very successful project. And some of those young people, who normally stood on the street corners and wouldn't attend the youth club, were encouraged, through the caravan project, to come along and join in youth club activities.

And not only that, we brought peer educators to the caravan to speak to these young people. One of them, Jeanette Keenan, began to work alongside Stuart on a regular basis. Paddy McStravick also came along and talked to them about his football club and told them that they were all welcome to come and join in – Paddy now has seven football teams, involving all different age groups. Then he would have got the boxers up to talk to the young people: 'Look, if there's any of youse are getting into fights, why not come down and fight in the ring instead?' There was an AIDS awareness day and Stuart and some of the young people arranged to take the caravan to Corn Market in the city centre where they gave out leaflets about AIDS and other health matters. They would also park outside discos where they gave young people information on the dangers of drugs and other things. Unfortunately, the big problem with the caravan was finding somewhere it could be parked when not in use. Farset let us park it inside their gates, but somebody drove in one day, hooked it up and disappeared off with it! We never recovered it, and it was a really big loss.

The problem with the caravan was finding somewhere it could be parked when not in use. Farset let us park it inside their gates, but somebody drove in one day, hooked it up and disappeared off with it! It was a really big loss.

There was a young girl who used to shadow me, Louise Beck, and she was also involved in the Newhill Youth Development Team. We got involved, through Springboard, with Protestant young people from the Shankill and other young people from Leitrim, so it was cross-border as well as cross-community. We did this project called 'Tell it like it is', and Louise was the project leader on that. I would give her a bit of support but Louise really worked away by herself and did a really great job. The three groups of young people put together a joint exhibition – involving photographs, a website, display panels, etc. – reflecting their 'past, present and future'. It was put on in the Waterfront Hall, then in Leitrim. So that was another good project, with the end result being each group taking ownership of their contribution to the project.

Another thing I was involved in with another young girl who shadowed me, Shauna Carson, was called 'Keep it safe', and that was basically young people working with senior citizens. A local priest, Father Denny, had been beaten up and had his car stolen by some teenagers. And there was a whole outcry with people saying: 'Young people are this and that!' Shauna was looking for a project and I said to her: 'There's a project right on your doorstep.' So she organised a meeting with some senior citizens to discuss their concerns, and from that a whole project developed. She got a brochure printed which included input not only from the senior citizens, but from young people, the fire brigade, Help the Aged and others – and on the back page it had all these telephone numbers that senior citizens might find useful.

And in between all this work my family was growing up. I had two boys and three girls, and we were always a very close-knit family. They have taken a lot of interest in my work, and would even have become involved. For although you were doing so much work in the community you still had to leave time for your own family. They were always first and foremost, and I managed to balance it very well. As they were growing up they would have been members of the youth club, or they would have been going to the youth club on the nights that I was there. And when I wasn't in the house Tommy, my husband, was there for them,

> *For although you were doing so much work in the community you still had to leave time for your own family. They were always first and foremost, and I managed to balance it very well.*

so they were always looked after. And this was despite the fact that community and youth work can be very challenging and time-consuming. I mean, you might say that you were going 'up there' for two hours, but be away for four hours, you know. One daughter, Deirdre, works in the community, and another, Louise, used to work for BRO and different clubs. My eldest son, Thomas, returned to education then went to university to study computer engineering. Robert is a roofer and Maria is an auxiliary nurse. I've ten grandchildren: the oldest is 20 and the youngest is seven months.

Anyway, when the ACE jobs finished you were left with a greatly reduced workforce. We would maybe have had a full-time worker or a part-time worker for each of the different projects, and then perhaps four ACE workers. But when that all went you were left with only one staff member, and were wondering where you could get the money to bring in sufficient workers to cater for the needs of the local children and young people. But we always struggled on, trying to get funding from different places.

And you were always glad when you got opportunities to take the young people away out of the area to places that didn't cost that much. Like Kinder Community House in Killough, which was very inexpensive. For a couple of years I was on the management committee which was set up to run the Kinder House.† Kinder Community House was absolutely brilliant. I think we were one of the first groups to use it. See one of the first times we went away, I had a

---

† *Editor's note:* In 1974 the Dutch charity, Pax Christi Kinderhulp (PCK), began taking 120 Northern Irish children to Holland for three weeks each summer. In 1988, having raised a substantial amount of money, PCK asked me to investigate what this funding could best be used for. I interviewed 20 community groups, Newhill among them, and the consensus was that the money be used to purchase a residential venue. A suitable property was found in Killough, Co Down, and that venue is still going strong. PCK, while no longer taking children to Holland, is still very involved in Northern Ireland. For some anecdotes about the Kinder House, see Island Pamphlet No. 59, *'Home and Away: some reminiscences on community-based children's holiday projects'*.

real laugh. It was a young women's group, they were going to be peer educators and it was like a training weekend. There were 12 young women in the group: 15- and 16-year-old young 'ladies'. And you know what they're like at that age – they wanted to look all glamorous, and they *were*, they were beautiful. Anyway, the minibus stopped outside the Kinder House. Now, the exterior of the Kinder House has drab stonework, and from the front the house itself can look small. This was all slightly off-putting to the girls. 'Is that where we're going?' they said. 'We're not going in there!' Then the caretaker, Jack, came over from across the road and opened the door.... And you walked into this lovely hall and stairway and you could see into one room with its big fireplace, and another door leading into an extensive kitchen and dining area. And when the group explored the house they were surprised at how big it was. With two reception rooms we were able to use those to split the group in two. We went down in May and the weather was fantastic. Most of the workshops actually took place in the big, deep gardens at the back, which ran right down to the beach. And in the evenings we would tell ghost stories in the larger of the two living rooms and eat pizzas or sandwiches.

Kinder Community House was absolutely brilliant... [One time] we went down in May and the weather was fantastic. Most of the workshops actually took place in the big, deep gardens at the back, which ran right down to the beach. And in the evenings we would tell ghost stories in the larger of the two living rooms and eat pizzas or sandwiches.

And when we got back to Belfast the girls all asked: 'Right, when are we going back there?' We could have used that place every month. We used it for an awful lot of training. We brought down different age groups, and we did drama workshops. And the kids loved it, so they did. And, as I said, at that particular time Newhill never had much money and the Kinder House was so inexpensive. The house was warm and inviting, and Killough village itself was beautiful, especially if you got good weather. The owner of the pub next door used to make us a big pot of soup or a big tray of chips – we would have paid him, of course. That was a great help, because it meant you could have prepared a load of sandwiches and you'd soup and all made for you to go with them. So we thought it was absolutely brilliant. And it was also a great place if you wanted to bring away your youth leaders for a training weekend, for it meant that they were near home. Because a couple of times we would have been away somewhere and maybe one of the leaders got word, 'Oh, you have to come home, such and such has happened.' And Killough was only three-quarters of an hour's drive away.

I was also on the committee of the Community Arts Forum. We got Janice Kennedy, a drama lecturer in Jordanstown, to come down to Killough with one of the younger groups to do a play. I stayed with the Community Arts Forum for a right few years, and there were great things going on there too. You met all these Spanish flamenco dancers, and salsa dancers, and we got all our young group involved with all the different arts and dances – it was great.

Volunteers from American, Belgium, Holland, Finland and England have also helped out in our summer schemes in Newhill. Local people put them up for the three weeks they were here, and some have remained in contact with us.

Cross-community contact is another thing which is important for our young people. In the peer education project there was a young Protestant fella from the Shankill, Gary, who was employed as one of the peer educators, and he worked up here. And another young fella was on an art project, and he had a friend from the Shankill and the two of them worked together on similar projects and would have come together to share their experiences. One or two Protestant boys played for Newhill in our football club. So for manys a day we have been doing cross-community work. When we were doing the 'Tell it like it is' project with Springboard – alongside the young people from the Shankill and Leitrim – when we all first met we split up into three workshops And we were all just looking at each other and I think we recognised that everything was getting glossed over. A girl from the Shankill, Gail, said: 'This is all very nice, but...' And I says, 'You're right, I think if we're going to do this project properly it has to be warts and all.' So we talked about our differences and we discussed various contentious issues, but we still accepted each other's cultures, and we managed to bring it all together into one big project.

Paul Lappin, as Leader in Charge of Newhill, worked with a group of young Protestant fellas from an equally disadvantaged area, with high unemployment and similar circumstances to ours. And our young people also went to meet a group of young people in Liverpool who were from a disadvantaged area too.

Over the years we have worked on many projects, we've also done training in 'single identity', looking at our own culture and the symbols of that culture, then looking at what we perceived the 'other' community's culture to be, and what *their* emblems might represent. We would have gone away for weekends to Rostrevor with groups from the West Circular Road, and got them all to work together. So for a long time we have been working with groups from other communities. But you'd find that you're there for the weekend

Sometimes you saw a young person taking off their Rangers shirt and giving it to one of our young people and them going home with a Celtic shirt.

and everybody's gelling together and then when the kids depart they'll shout, you know, something like.... 'Up the UDA!' or 'Up the 'RA'!' And you say to yourself: like, we were great all weekend and now look at all this stuff! But, having said that, sometimes you saw a young person taking off their Rangers shirt and giving it to one of our young people and them going home with a Celtic shirt. There was an awful lot of effort put in over the years to create

26

conditions in which young people from both communities could come together in neutral venues and discuss the problems that they all face.

Nobody likes to be in a war situation and I never liked it. I just hope that although terrible things have happened that now we're all trying to work together, and trying to give our young people a better future than what we had. For I would never like to see my grandchildren going through what my children had to go through and witness. But at present it's still up and down; hopefully it will even itself out and we will be able to live with each other in peace and harmony.

I'm glad that there'll be peace, although God knows how long it will take before there's complete peace, because every morning you get up you hear of some breakdown in law and order; look at the incidents that have occurred recently: the stabbings and the rapes. And although the police were never welcome in these areas because of all that happened, there's a definite need in these areas for a police service that everyone can trust. As I said, you get up every morning and you look at the newspaper and it's just sickening to read about yet another young person being stabbed. I have always had great hopes for young people and they are the future, so we have to trust that they have it in them. But then again, have we been good role models? I think the young people *will* make the effort, you know, and there will be a better future.

> *I just hope that although terrible things have happened that now we're all trying to work together, and trying to give our young people a better future than what we had. For I would never like to see my grandchildren going through what my children had to go through and witness.*

When I worked with young people there was a lot of them who had almost no self-esteem. I always let young people know: don't ever be afraid to speak out in case you say anything stupid, for it's the only way you're going to learn, and if you do make mistakes, don't worry, you can talk about it and learn from it. I always wanted to build confidence in young people.

And lack of self-confidence is a major problem – and you can see that especially through the recent increase in youth suicides. A number of young people from our area have died through suicide, and it's very, very worrying. It's so heartbreaking... I've been at a couple of these young people's funerals and just looking at their parents, looking at their wee friends... and then the next thing you hear is that one of their wee friends has done the same, you know. A young girl in our area was knocked down and killed by a stolen car, and her brother later died through suicide. Then, on top of that, coming up to *his* anniversary, his girlfriend died though suicide as well, God love her.

I have no idea what way you could actually solve this problem, but what I think could go a long way in helping to tackle it would be adequate resources and funding. There is a terrible lack of facilities in this area to cope with the problems that young people face. For instance, a young fella from the Cashmere Road died through suicide in his friend's house recently, and he had been waiting four months to see a counsellor. Now, if a young person has problems, a day is a long time to wait to talk to anybody. His father wrote a letter which was read out by other parents, and in it he encouraged young people to talk. And I think they need to talk, they need to have somewhere to go, to know that they can trust people who are going to listen to their problems.

Now, you can't say to a young person, 'I'm going to solve your problems', for ultimately that young person has to resolve things themselves. But you can be there to support that young person and you can say: I can put you in touch with people who you need to go to. But you also need to feel confident that those facilities are actually there before you even say such things. They weren't definitely there when I first began working with young people.

When I would listen to the young people quite a few of them had big personal problems, and not only that, there were many young people who were afraid of getting into trouble with paramilitaries, or afraid of getting into trouble with drug dealers and all the rest of it. And there were some young people who were self-harming themselves and things like that, and it was a big worry.

Confidentially is a big issue too. When you know that somebody is coming to you, to tell you something in confidence, you have to say to that young person: Look, if you're going to tell me about something that I think is going to endanger you in any way, I'm going to have to go and try and get you whatever type of support you need. The problem is that that support is not always out there, or if it *is* out there it's not staring you in the face. I think young people *will* talk, if the facilities are there, and if they know where to go to, but the government has to put money into resources. Resources to assist young people – and, indeed, the wider community – with suicide awareness and drugs awareness. I always said to the young people when I was working with them: 'Look, nothing will ever shock me, so don't be afraid to tell me anything, I'll listen, and if there's any way at all I can give you support I'll do it.' Some young people

Some young people will come forward, but others will never come forward. So there's this whole thing about young people who need help but don't seek it, and it's how you get them to open up and begin talking about their problems.

will come forward, but others will never come forward. So there's this whole thing about young people who need help but don't seek it, and it's how you get them to open up and begin talking about their problems.

We once brought a lot of young people together from all the clubs and we did YES – Youth Empowerment Scheme – which was basically for the young people to do a survey on themselves and with other young people. And it was asking them: what are your needs, what will stop you from getting into trouble, what will stop you from hanging around corners, what will stop you from doing this, that or the other... And what came out of it was that most wanted somewhere to go, they wanted to be in a place where they could just sit and talk. And that's what we had always wanted with Newhill. Somewhere they could have a bit of craic, that would just take them away from the street corners. And we had some great wee nights, even in the days when it was freezing and we all huddled around the gas heaters, and you'd have seen a group sitting there warming themselves up, talking about all different subjects, all full of fun and craic. And you could tell that they thought: 'This is our place, this is where we can go to meet and talk.'

And it doesn't take you to be the most fantastic youth leader in the world to be able to listen. The very fact that young people know that you're there for them, and you're allowing them to speak and you're empathizing with them in the situation that they're in is so important. And they'll know, by the way you're listening, whether you're really taking in what they're saying.

And we had some great wee nights, even in the days when it was freezing and we all huddled around the gas heaters, and you'd have seen a group sitting there warming themselves up, talking about all different subjects, all full of fun and craic.

We used drama to bring young people out of themselves. The young people in Newhill wrote this play called 'Teenage Kicks', and it was absolutely fantastic. They wrote it themselves and put it on in the Group Theatre. It was only on for one night, but we could have had it there for a week because the response they got was brilliant. And within that play the young people addressed a range of issues: there was a pregnancy, there was a death connected to drugs, there was someone suffering from low-esteem... So they know what they want to talk about. And with young people who can't always share their problems or show their emotions, getting them involved in drama and role-playing – where they can take on a different character, act a different person – helps to bring them out of themselves. We'd a young fella involved in the youth club who had a really tough time growing up, and we got him involved in drama. He won this wee trophy and he was so delighted with it! Now, I'm talking about an 18-year-old and he was saying: 'I can't get over this... I have won this!' I used to worry about this young person, but drama helped to bring him round, and got him to mix better. And through role-playing and drama young people were maybe acting out part of their lives, getting rid of things which they couldn't come straight out and say to you... but they could write it down and let on it was somebody else. But by playing that role they were actually, I'm not saying freeing themselves completely, but they were indirectly telling their story. So I think that the likes of drama therapy is great for young people.

I always found that the majority of young people I worked with *wanted* to be involved, you know, wanted to be included in everything that was going on. When you said to them, 'What do you think of this situation?' some of them would look at you and reply: 'Are you actually asking me what I think about this, do you want me to tell you?' 'Yes, I want you to tell me.' 'But will you listen?' 'Yes, I'll listen.' 'But will you do anything about it?' 'If what you suggest is realistic, yes.' I would say to them: 'You can try to do something, and if it doesn't happen you can always say: well, at least I did my best to make this happen.'

We have always recognised that in Newhill our greatest strength is the people in our community and the support we get from them – and I'm including the people all around: Dermot Hill, New Barnsley.... At every occasion possible, we try to keep the community spirit alive. When I was in the youth club you could recognise different talents in the young people. As the years passed these young people were leaving, getting jobs, or starting to go out with boyfriends or girlfriends and eventually stopped coming to the youth club. But maybe a few years later we would have contacted them and said, 'Look, we remember you were a great dancer, we need you to come up and teach the young kids some dancing.' Or 'You were great at drama, we need you to come up and do that again.' So the young people who had first encountered Newhill as members were coming back and working as leaders, and that's the way it has continued. Indeed, some of our first members are now on the management committee. Three of them – Tracie McKee, Rosie McCrory and Caren Conlon – all work with our young people in the area of creative arts, making sure that all young people's talents are provided with a creative outlet, whether that be art, dance, drama or music.

So we try and keep the whole community involved, we try to maintain their interest and that caring atmosphere about the project. For although our focus has been on children and young people, the whole community needs support. I was saying earlier about kids who didn't leave the area; well, there were plenty of adults who didn't venture outside these areas either. You just didn't travel the way you used to travel before the Troubles. The main place in your life *was* your community, so you had to build up your community to meet *all* your needs.

There were plenty of adults who didn't venture outside these areas either. You just didn't travel the way you used to travel before the Troubles. The main place in your life was your community, so you had to build up your community to meet all your needs.

Now... I'm thinking back on my own life and saying, 'How did I get involved in all this?' And I don't think if there hadn't been a war situation here I would ever have got so involved. Indeed, I might never have been involved at all, because I never, ever thought I'd end up working with young people as a youth worker – and the generation gap made no difference whatsoever. But I think it was because there was a need, a definite need there, not only for somewhere for my own children to go, but for all the young people in this area to go, something for them to do, keep them occupied and somewhere to socialise.

I think women came to the forefront and did an awful lot of community work. In fact, when I started out it was nearly *all* women doing community work, partly because so many men were in jail at that particular time. I mean, I had two brothers on the 'blanket protest' – one of whom, Joe, died on hunger strike – and my own husband was interned. That was just one family – and there were many families affected the same way. There were an awful lot of years when women were left to bring up their children themselves, and not only that, but they had to learn new skills for themselves. Things they might previously have left their husbands to do they now had to do for themselves. So women were to the forefront of community work. At one particular time in Newhill it was *all* women.

On reflection, as a woman who was initially hesitant to get involved in youth work, I now see all those years as having greatly enriched my life. Whatever I was able to give to young people – and I hope it has been of value to them – they have given me even more in return.

Whatever I was able to give to young people – and I hope it has been of value to them – they have given me even more in return.